T 19

I
SHOULD
BE
WRITING

I
SHOULD
BE
WRITING

—

A WRITER'S
WORKSHOP

Mur Lafferty

ROCK
POINT
QUARTOKNOWS.COM

Brimming with creative inspiration, how-to projects, and useful information to enrich your everyday life, Quarto Knows is a favorite destination for those pursuing their interests and passions. Visit our site and dig deeper with our books into your area of interest: Quarto Creates, Quarto Cooks, Quarto Homes, Quarto Lives, Quarto Drives, Quarto Explores, Quarto Gifts, or Quarto Kids.

First published in 2017 by Rock Point, an imprint of The Quarto Group,
142 West 36th Street, 4th Floor, New York, NY 10018, USA
T (212) 779-4972 F (212) 779-6058 **www.QuartoKnows.com**

Rock Point titles are also available at discount for retail, wholesale, promotional, and bulk purchase. For details, contact the Special Sales Manager by email at specialsales@quarto.com or by mail at The Quarto Group, Attn: Special Sales Manager, 401 Second Avenue North, Suite 310, Minneapolis, MN 55401, USA.

10 9 8 7 6 5 4 3 2

ISBN: 978-1-63106-365-7

Editorial Director: Rage Kindelsperger
Creative Director: Merideth Harte
Managing Editor: Erin Canning
Editorial Project Manager: Chris Krovatin
Cover and Interior Design: Jen Cogliantry

Printed in China

MIX
Paper from
responsible sources
FSC
www.fsc.org   FSC® C104723

For Jennifer Greer Brady
and Richard Dansky,
both of whom wouldn't let me give up
at different times in my life.

And to my podcast listeners, without
whom this wouldn't have happened.

CONTENTS

Introduction

When I was a child, I wrote a bunch of stories and my teacher stapled them together and wrote 'STORIES' on the cover. A few years later, I started my first book. It starred all of my friends as characters who each had our own different colored unicorn to ride as we fought evil. In a fit of writerly rage, I threw it away into the trash can. My best friend Jennifer rescued it.

Incidentally, Stephen King has a similar story regarding his wife Tabitha rescuing his early manuscript for *Carrie* from the trash. I like that King and I share an origin story even though my unicorn story and *Carrie* soon diverged in their paths. That's probably for the best.

Soon after, I was a terrified freshman in a high school where no one noticed me. Our stern, kinda scary science teacher, Mr. Webb, challenged us to write a science fiction short story called "A Day without Light." We then had to stand up in front of the class and read them. I didn't look up from my story once when I read it aloud, my voice shaking. Then everyone had a secret ballot to vote for the best one. To my utter shock, mine won. (People still didn't talk to me much, though)

Throughout the rest of high school, Mr. Webb amused himself by saying, "Look up, Mur!" every time he saw me. He wasn't so scary anymore.

In college, I took an independent study class with the late Southern writer Doris Betts. I loved that class because it had people weirder than me. It also had people better than me. The person who intimidated me the most was Dan Kois. This was in my own head, of course; Dan was a sweetheart. (Dan writes for *Slate* now. Good for you, Dan!)

People better than me? This was discouraging on a level that I shouldn't have allowed. After college, I got a job and stopped writing.

Why did I quit, really? It's hard to say, not because I don't know, but because I don't like admitting it. But admitting is what inspired this book, so here goes: I quit because I was done with school, and I didn't think I could ever get any better, and since people like those in my class were better than I was, then, I thought, *I might as well not try anymore.*

I saw writing as a destination, not a journey. If I wasn't a writer by the end of school, then I had reached the end of my development and would never improve.

I still dreamed of writing "one day." I didn't know when that day would come, of course. If you're reading this book, then it's likely you know that magical "someday." You probably have your own nebulous time in the future when you will sit down and follow your dreams. Not today, but, you know, someday.

A few years later, I met Richard Dansky, a writer of role-playing games and gothic horror. He offered to become my mentor to get me writing again. He made me realize how many years I had wasted. I started writing fiction again.

A few years later, I heard the word *podcasting* for the first time. I soon created a show where I read some of the nonfiction geeky essays I'd been working on. I began to build an audience.

A few months after that, I met the man who created the first writing podcast (to my knowledge), fantasy author Michael A. Stackpole. Mike was giving his sage, experienced advice to newbies, usually reproducing his popular newsletter in audio form. I thought it was a great show, but I wondered what would happen if someone did a podcast for newbies by a newbie. I asked Mike whether he minded if I did a show on writing.

Aside: The idea of asking permission to create a podcast on an already existing theme is gut-bustingly laughable today, when there are hundreds of thousands of podcasts. But (as far as I knew) I was creating the second writing podcast that existed. It felt natural to check with the person who did the first one.

Anyway, Mike gave me his blessing to make another show. Titles aren't my strong point, and I struggled with what to call a show that was by a beginner, for a beginner. My friend, author and podcaster Tee Morris, suggested calling it "I Should Be Writing" (ISBW for short). My new show debuted in August 2005. Podcasting was one year old and almost no one had heard of it. Even iTunes had only just begun to support it.

I began recording my hopes, my fears, my dreams, and my setbacks, giving people an honest view of a beginning writer's life— someone who could easily be discouraged but wasn't going to give up. I focused not so much on the craft, because I was a newbie there. But I did know the brain weasels (or the bullies, which we will talk about later in this book) that will eat away at a writer, and how those weasels lie. These lies say the editor who rejected you will never publish you. They say you're on a blacklist. They say no matter how hard you work, you'll never get better. They say that when you have a gorgeous perfect idea and it doesn't look perfect on the page, it means that there is something wrong with you. I addressed the lies, struggled on my end, and kept writing.

I sold some short stories, self-published some audio fiction via podcast, and then got a book deal from Orbit six years after launching ISBW.

In 2015 I was inducted into the Podcaster Hall of Fame. In 2016 I started writing this book.

My show, and now this book, was designed mainly to tell you that *you are not alone*. The fears that plague you, the walls you hit, and nearly every problem you encounter trying to publish has been experienced by every writer: new, veteran, best sellers, and mid-listers.

I am here to tell you not to quit. Don't lose years off your writing life for no better reason than "I'm not good enough." If you keep writing, you'll get better.

You should be writing.

Mur Lafferty
November 26, 2016
Buffalo, New York

CHAPTER 1

Acorn Writers, Oak Expectations

Every writer suffers from the imposter syndrome from time to time—some more often! Of course, new writers worry that they don't have what it takes, but did you know that well-published writers worry about whether they've lost what it takes? Self-doubt never goes away, although I think maybe that's not a bad thing. It certainly keeps me from getting complacent! But I find that these concerns are most acute when I'm not writing. When I'm writing, even if things aren't going well, I know that I'm doing the best I can. So sit down and get to it! "

— James Patrick Kelly,
award-winning science-fiction and fantasy author

I get a lot of email from listeners with themes. I think one of the most prevalent messages is from people who are hesitant to call themselves writers.

And it's tough. With a science-based job, you can call yourself a doctor or an engineer or a biologist or an astronomer when you graduate from years of school. With blue-collar work, you can call yourself a barista, a construction worker, or a ditch digger, when you get hired and trained. Sometimes you need education or certification.

The common thing between a doctor and a plumber is *you aren't one until someone else tells you.*

But no one tells you when you're finally an artist, a dancer, or a writer. Yeah, you can get jobs, or schooling, but there are people who have never had any training at all and they still are writers, and actors, and singers.

We're so used to someone else marking our finish lines that we aren't sure what to do when no one has marked out the course. Where do you start? How do you manage obstacles? Where do you finish and say you're finally A Writer?

One of the saddest things I read in my email is people telling me that they don't want to call themselves writers yet, or that their family or friends ask them when they're going to start publishing and make the "big bucks."

This is unfair to the extreme. If you were to start a running program, would your family and friends say, "So have you run a marathon yet?" No, they would say, "You did a half mile today? Awesome!"

If you wanted to be a surgeon, they wouldn't say, "How come you're not doing brain surgery yet?" They would say, "Biology and chemistry this semester? Smart."

Or that's what they would say, you know . . . if they aren't jerks.

Nearly every skill or profession has a learning curve. Just like a beginning baker needs to learn about what baking soda does, or a beginning accountant needs to understand the tax code, so a beginning writer needs to understand the three-act structure of a story or how to build a complex character. And just like an athlete needs to work out frequently to achieve any success, a writer must write. A lot.

Still, it's hard to tell when you've reached the level you're aspiring to. There is no test; there is no final exam. No one can tell you that you graduated and now get to make a living writing. We get better by increments and continue to evolve through our whole creative career, which is both good and frustrating. If there is no official person who says, "You're good enough," then you will always wonder: am I a writer?

Let's skip over that whole bucket of angst. You're a writer.

Now keep reading.

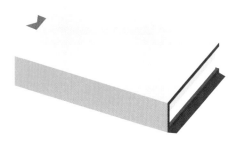

IMPOSTER SYNDROME

Imposter syndrome is often unexpected (I certainly didn't see it coming), but it's surprisingly common. When almost anyone starts to achieve success or improvement or just starts getting attention for something they posted on a fanfic site, they start to feel uneasy. They don't feel *different*. Nothing has changed for them, and yet suddenly others say they're a writer. But in their head, they're not a real writer like Patterson, Rowling, Gaiman, Butler, etc. They just wrote that thing, the one that people happen to like, and those people are probably wrong anyway.

In 2011 I had to pleasure of interviewing Lev Grossman, author of the series *The Magicians* (the books that show is based on). His second book had just come out and that morning it had hit the *New York Times* best-seller list. Before the interview started I congratulated him on the news, and he looked down at the floor and said, in a tight monotone, "Thank you, it's very exciting." He looked like I had asked if he felt ready to roll a giant boulder up a hill.

BULLY: *You've got imposter syndrome just like Lev? I know Lev Grossman. And you, sir/madam/nonbinary, are no Lev Grossman.*

MUSE: *We don't need another Lev. Lev's identical twin, author Austin Grossman, isn't even Lev! Lev is already Lev. You need to be the best YOU you can be, compared to no one else.*

Lev said he was still waiting for people to come to their senses and return all the books and demand their money back.

Later that night he won the John W. Campbell Award for Best New Writer.

Lev is definitely the real thing. He wrote a compelling series that people loved, was a best seller, and became a hit television show. But he felt like an imposter that day, waiting for people to come to his door with pitchforks and call him out for daring to pretend to be a real writer.

The thing is, getting an agent, publishing a book, becoming a best seller, or getting an award—none of that can erase imposter syndrome. The feeling comes from the inside, and nothing external can touch it.

Well, something can touch it. People can make imposter syndrome worse with bad reviews or rude comments online (or worse, in person!). It's a depressing aspect of human nature that makes us value negative comments more than positive comments. I think it's because the negative comments reinforce our greatest fears, no matter how illogical.

So what do you do? You do what you do with most every writerly anxiety: you get back to work. The time and effort you spend under the (real or metaphorical) blanket fort, worrying that people are going to find you out, could better be used writing your next story.

ONE MILLION WORDS

Malcolm Gladwell made famous the rule that to become an expert, you must spend ten thousand hours on your passion. It is also sometimes listed as ten years.

Ray Bradbury said you have to write one million words of crap, get it all out of your system, before anything good comes out.

These numbers (ten thousand hours, ten years, and one million words)

BULLY: *That's ten long years of bills to pay. Why waste your time?*

MUSE: *If you write for the next ten years, you'll be the same age as if you hadn't written! And you'll be a much better writer for it.*

are arbitrary, and were created because humans like big, round numbers. The point is, excelling at anything takes a lot of work. It takes setbacks and learning and plateaus and frustrations and being absolutely sure you will never, ever publish anything. It takes looking at other people's careers and thinking that they have it easy, that they are lucky, that they are perfect and you are crap.

The reality is, other people's careers have likely had the setbacks and learning curves and plateaus that you've experienced. You just don't see that when you look at them. You see their amazing book, their awards, and their long autograph line. You haven't seen their years of struggling and haven't read their terrible words that came before they published anything.

I was getting work writing early in my career, but that was for

role-playing games. It used a lot of the same muscles as fiction writing, but was still vastly different. It took me writing for three more years after my first role-playing game job to sell a story. After that it took me five more years to sell a book to a major publisher—and then the book didn't come out until 18 months *after* that.

People who seem to be overnight successes just haven't been on your radar. They keep their blood, sweat, and tears to themselves and only appear in front of you when they succeed. In your eyes, they're the goddess Athena, bursting fully grown in awesome glory from Zeus's head.

> **BULLY:** *Zeus never should have eaten Athena's mother: that's all there is to it.*

> **MUSE:** *You're not usually one to consider the effects of an action.*

> **BULLY:** *That was before a demigoddess started making armor for her daughter inside my head.*

In a lot of "successful" writers' eyes, they're a very tired mountain climber who just reached the summit of their personal mountain, only to see several taller mountains on the horizon.

It's a long journey. And yes, it's been a long journey for nearly everyone you admire.

THE COLD SHOWER OF TRUTH

I'm going to give you the bad news early. You should hear it. Even if you get a huge book deal next week, you'll still make more money doing a regular job for at least a few years.

Don't quit your day job.

Let me break it down for you. You get a six-figure deal for a trilogy and you're made in the shade, right? Write the boss a rude letter and dance out the door!

Wait.

If you sell a trilogy, the money will pay out kind of like this:

DATE	ADVANCE PAYMENT	ACTUAL
January Year 1	33 percent signing advance for books 1–3	33 percent of total advance
May Year 1	33 percent advance of book 1 for final draft	11 percent of total advance
November Year 1	33 percent advance of book 1 for publication	11 percent of total advance
May Year 2	33 percent advance of book 2 for final draft	11 percent of total advance
November Year 2	33 percent advance of book 2 for publication	11 percent of total advance
May Year 3	33 percent advance of book 3 for final draft	11 percent of total advance
November Year 3	33 percent advance of book 3 for publication	11 percent of total advance

Year one has a payday of 55 percent of your total advance, which is pretty sweet. You can live on that. But look at years two and three, where you make only 22 percent of the total advance each year. If you quit your day job, you'll have nothing else until you earn out that advance and start making royalties. And we didn't factor in your agent's cut (usually 15 percent) or taxes (usually 30 percent in the United States), which the

BULLY: *Just quit now, pal! You'll never make a living doing this!*

MUSE: *Money can't be your only goal! The point is, keep writing! Don't quit!*

publisher won't hold back. That's your job.

Taking all of that that into consideration, you will take home roughly half the advance ... over three years. And who knows when the next paycheck will come?

So what the heck do we do this for? If money is the brass ring for most writers, and this job still won't support you even after you start selling, then what's the point?

It's that we love it. We love making art, we love writing, we love telling stories. These stories will run around our head if we don't let them out, so we might as well see if we can get paid for our passion.

No matter how much money you make, you will have told a story. And that's awesome.

CHAPTER 2

YOUR TOOLS

> I wish someone had told me that having your first novel published isn't the end of the slog. It's the beginning of a tougher journey. No one wants to say this to new writers because the process of being an emerging writer is demoralizing enough as it is, and most never make it as far as a first completed novel, let alone a published one. But while that may seem like the single hurdle you need to jump to have a successful career, it's just the first, and the lowest, barrier in the profession... "

> **—Kameron Hurley,**
> science-fiction and fantasy author and essayist

So you've made it past the cold reality of being a writer and are on to actually getting some stuff done. Good for you! You're a warrior and stronger than most people who dream of that "someday."

What do you need to be a writer? Pen and paper, duh! Sure, but there are many, many other tools out there that can help you get down to actually doing the work.

TOOLS YOU HAVE
Your Muse & Your Bully

Like it or not, these are already alive and active inside your head. Maybe they're an angel and a devil. Maybe one is a supportive fairy and the other a lurking basement monster. Maybe one is a beloved relative and the other has the face of a mean teacher from your past. But I'm betting you have anthropomorphized the muse, the place in your subconscious that gives you your ideas. Your muse is someone who goes out to play when you're doing mindless chores, or walking, or sometimes reading stories by someone else. It gets active and then suddenly you have A Big Idea.

How many times have you been showering, or driving, or cleaning, or doing a jigsaw puzzle, and suddenly an idea burst into your head? Your muse is at work here, and it is very happy to have time to juggle some ideas and pick the best. The lesson is that you must give your brain some downtime to let the muse come out and play. If you spend all your time using your brain, whether at your day job or staring at your computer screen, then your muse will stay locked up. You have to let it out on occasion. Then it will flourish.

MUSE: *That's me! Have I got some ideas for you!*

Now we come to the other one. It's often called the "inner editor" because it looks at your story critically while you're writing it, interrupting the creative flow with pointless questions about word usage or sentence structure. I prefer the term *bully*, though. An editor works with you, at the right time, to make the story better. A bully uses your fears and worries against you to distract you while you're trying to write.

Now we aren't saying your work won't need edits. Remember that your first draft won't be perfect, and you will want to give a critical eye to it once you are done. But the time to edit your work is on rewrite, not first draft. And striving for perfection can ruin your goal of finishing; perfection is impossible, and if you wait for perfection, then you will never finish your story and send it out.

BETWEEN YOU AND ME: I hate absolutes in writing advice. When it comes to editing while writing, many pros write very clean first drafts, or finish their day's writing and then go through and edit. Or they edit yesterday's work before starting on today's. The "do not edit until you're done" rule is for people who really do take hours (or even days) making sure their first sentence is as perfect as it can be before moving on to the next one. That way lies madness.

Physical Tools

It's tempting to get the newest and shiniest program and notebook and pen and computer and tablet and smartphone to start your writing career. But that's the bully talking, a clever distraction to keep you from actually working on your craft.

> **BULLY:** *You should go online and buy the super expensive notebook and the fancy fountain pen and don't write one word until they get here. Your art deserves such luxury, and you shouldn't go without.*

> **MUSE:** *Or you could get a pencil and the back of an envelope and jot down some ideas, and get a legal pad and a pack of pens for less than a lunch out and get to work. That is good, too.*

> **BULLY:** *Is that a My Little Pony notebook? Really?*

> **MUSE:** *While you were insulting Applejack, I got another chapter written.*

If you prefer longhand, you need something to write with. This will be a pen or a pencil—not a fountain pen and not a shiny new pack of pencils. I'm sure you have something lying around your house.

Then you need paper: a notebook you buy at the dollar store is enough. You don't need a fancy $20 notebook. Heck, we have pages in this book where you can practice. That's money saved!

Too many people (and I've been guilty of this) think that they must have the fanciest paper and pen in order to feel like a real writer. I have countless beautiful blank books. When I really want to get ideas down, though, I grab a yellow legal pad. The pad gives me less pressure to put brilliance into its forever-bound pages. If I don't like what I write, I rip it out and throw it away. My scrawled bad ideas don't live in the pretty book forever.

As for other tools, most people these days have at least access to a computer. Several free word-processing programs currently exist. They include Google Drive, Open Office, or the programs probably bundled with your computer, like Apple Pages for Mac. You can also write on your tablet if you have one.

At the very least, you can type an email to yourself into your smartphone and put your writing in there. I've done this. It ain't pretty, but it works.

Although writers are not the flashiest breed of artists in general, we certainly have the lowest threshold to enter. You don't need a musical instrument or paint or a sketchbook or dance shoes. So that excuse is crumbled. Get to work.

Technology & Education

If your handwriting is so horrible that even you can't read it after writing a particularly exciting scene, then writing a chapter by hand is definitely out. If you're not on a shoestring budget, what tools should you get?

For good word-processing programs that you can buy, the favorites are Microsoft Word (pretty much the publishing standard) and Scrivener.

Word is the behemoth, it's been around forever, and *everyone* uses it. It's for everyone, though, and is bloated with bells and whistles most writers don't need: graphic design tools, tables, charts, image placement and so on. You will probably need it if you work with a professional editor, but it's not every writer's favorite tool.

Scrivener is a program built for writers of books and short stories. It allows you to do character sketches, keep scenes separate, move said scenes around as if they were index cards on your office floor, and more. I'm not being paid by Scrivener to say this; I'm just a big fan. This book was written using Scrivener, incidentally. The program is available on Mac, Windows, and iOS.

So what about education? Can you do this alone or should you get a creative writing degree? Join an expensive workshop? Get an MFA?

First, academics. If you're in an undergrad or graduate program, classes and workshops can teach you a lot about craft, and how to critique well, which is a skill that will improve your own writing more than you think. Finding like-minded writers on your own level is an asset that shouldn't be overlooked. You can definitely benefit from learning from a professional instructor, too.

The downsides to academic study are that some teachers and other students may try to critique your work into being more like their own, instead of urging it to the best story you can write. Some programs may not welcome your genre of writing if you're not writing literary fiction.

(I have a master's degree, but some people look disappointed when I say it's in popular fiction instead of *literature*.)

The unfortunate truth is that while having a business or medical degree can take you far in a job hunt, having a writing degree doesn't guarantee you a book sale. But, speaking from experience, I would say the biggest pitfall of studying writing academically is that you might be better off studying topics that teach you about the world. If you study a wide range of things in school, it will allow you to write about a wide range of topics. Learning about how people interact via history, sociology, or anthropology will make your stories stronger. Knowledge of math and science can add realism to your work.

Knowing how stories are told is very important, but you also need to be able to understand what you're writing about when you're writing.

BULLY: *Meh. That's what Wikipedia is for*

MUSE: *Oh no, never use Wikipedia as your only reference tool! It once told me that Bubblegum won the Kentucky Derby!*

BULLY: *Bubblegum did win at 20-1 odds in 1985, I remember. I was there. My mother wore a huge hat.*

MUSE: *This never happened.*

Sometimes you will come across an opportunity to attend intensive conferences and workshops. In science fiction, for example, we have Clarion and Odyssey workshops, both six weeks, and Viable Paradise, one week. If you can spare the time and money, then I'd say go for it. Those kinds of workshops have been described to be life changing, and many successful authors today are graduates.

Conferences are excellent places to network, allowing you to talk to editors and agents and attend talks and smaller workshops. Do your research, though; many are expensive, so you should make sure you're getting your money's worth.

NaNoWriMo

National Novel Writing Month is a practice that started over a decade ago and has exploded in popularity. In November you can sign up to write a novel (well, 50,000 words) in thirty days. From day one to thirty, you need to write 1,666 words per day, and then you win . . . nothing. Bragging rights. Pride. A checkmark next to your name on the site.

An impossible thought, especially due to November containing perhaps the biggest U.S. travel holiday in the year, right?

Nope. It's huge. NaNoWriMo has gone from a one-month event to having a "camp" during the year where you just choose a project and work on it intently (with less stringent rules than NaNoWriMo), a Young Writers Program where they help out with writing programs in schools, and a forum for advice on what to do with the 50k words when you're done.

Many, many people use NaNoWriMo. There are write-ins run by local writers; there's a charity dinner in San Francisco (someday I will get out there to attend this). Beginners use to it get the experience of writing a large project without stress on quality because their only concern is word quantity, and pros do it to help jump-start projects. Authors who use NaNoWriMo include Mary Robinette Kowal (*Ghost Talkers*), Erin Morgenstern (*The Night Circus*), and Sara Gruen (*Water for Elephants*).

If you want a large community effort to light a fire under your writing butt, then NaNoWriMo is a great experience.

Unless you're reading this in March. If that's the case, then get to work regardless, dang it.

CHAPTER 3
Squashing Myths

> " Talent is a destructive myth. To call someone talented is to imply that their abilities are intrinsic. Having written and taught for decades now, I've satisfied myself that the improvement of a person's art isn't drawn from the mystical well of their soul: it's generated by practice. "
>
> **—Cory Doctorow,**
> award-winning science-fiction author and activist

The mysteries and myths surrounding writing can fly about and distract you from actually doing any real work. Irrational fears, romantic ideas about what a real writer is, or notions of what it takes to be a real writer—all of these can work to prevent you from writing a story or novel.

Bust the myths, and if they ever rear their heads again, then just get back to work.

IDEA THEFT

A lot of writers use a fear of other people "stealing their ideas" as an excuse to avoid sending out work, workshopping work, or even writing at all. Their ideas are precious jewels in their heads and they don't want anyone to even think of having access to them.

If someone else writes "my" book, then I can't write it, right?

Let me weave a rough plotline for you: a young woman who doesn't really stand out has something mysteriously special about her. She attracts the attention of a vampire. They fall madly in love and she becomes very powerful.

Did you think I was talking about *Twilight*? Or *Buffy the Vampire Slayer*? How about the Sookie Stackhouse novels (*True Blood* on television)? Robin McKinley's *Sunshine*? They all have this basic "idea" behind them, and yet they all are very different stories.

Let me say that plagiarism does exist. People steal from manuscripts. Movies and TV shows have been based on books that are a little too close to an existing novel (without having the rights to that novel). It happens. It goes to court. It can get ugly.

Not writing because you're afraid of plagiarists is like avoiding cars because of the possibility of dying in a car crash. But! We have a literary safety belt. It's called copyright.

You can't copyright an idea. If you could, we would very quickly run out of things to write about. If you give one writing prompt to thirty students, they will come up with thirty different stories. If someone "steals" your great idea, then you can bet her book/story will be different from yours.

As for the pros you will work with, agents and publishers don't want to steal from you. Agents make money when you make money. Stealing your idea doesn't make them any money. And frankly, it's a lot easier for a publisher to just give you a book deal than to jump through several sneaky hoops to steal from you and open themselves up to a lawsuit.

The fear of someone stealing an idea is an excuse. The seed of the excuse is fear. Don't let the fear control your writing future.

THE ROMANTIC, SICK AUTHOR

There is something romantic about being an author. We hear about authors who would smoke and drink and argue half the night and then write until sunup and then do it all again the next day. Or we hear that you must be tortured to write, and if you're not tortured, then you're doing it wrong.

BULLY: *Don't you want to be like Hemingway and Poe?*

MUSE: *I'd also like to avoid alcoholism and suicide. I want to live to be a healthy, old Muse.*

I'm not going to be pithy here. These are very dangerous myths. Many successful authors manage quite a nice output of work while being teetotalers. Most authors understand that a good night's sleep is good for your brain when you need to be creative. You don't need to put your body and mind through hell in order to properly write your story.

My least favorite myth is the one that says treating mental illness will stifle a writing career. People are afraid that depression and anxiety drugs will cut off their creativity. There are a lot of people who suffer needlessly through mental illness because of this fear.

Now, I am not a doctor. If you think you need something diagnosed, go see your doctor. But I will tell you that I battle depression, and it was getting very bad in 2004. That fall, I went on medication. A month later, I started podcasting and writing again. I had energy; my mind was clear and eager to create. I felt reborn.

There are many drugs on the market. Some, I've heard, do make you feel a bit more creatively dampened or slow. Others do not. You can do some research and talk to your doctor about what's right for you.

BULLY: *You sound like a medication commercial.*

> **MUSE:** *You should find out whether a specific drug is right for you! Do your research and ask questions! This is your life we're talking about!*

But here's the deal: your health is the most important thing. Take care of your health as best you can and then focus on the writing.

People say that if Van Gogh had been on medication, then he wouldn't have created as many amazing pieces of art. But heck, *so what*? Are we really prizing art over the health and well-being of a person? Would we damn others to mental illness in order for them to create for us?

Would Van Gogh have used mental illness meds if they'd been available? It's hard to say, as mental illness was more stigmatized then than it is now. But having the choice is the first step—you have the choice to get help, while he did not.

If you wouldn't do it to someone else, don't do it to yourself. Don't ignore problems and overindulge with alcohol or drugs because it's "romantic" and you want to be like Hemingway. Hemingway killed himself.

TALENT

Along the way, you will encounter people who have amazing talent. They will be able to causally toss off heartbreaking poems or make you fall in love with their characters in one sentence. You may wonder what the heck you're doing wasting your time, because you will never be that good.

BULLY: *You never WILL BE that good.*

MUSE: *Your job isn't to be as good as them. Your job is to be as good as or better than you were yesterday. I feel like I've said this before. I've said this before, right?*

Think about it this way: talent is like being tall. Tall people have an advantage in basketball, but if height were all you needed to play basketball, then all people over six feet tall would be basketball stars.

I will always remember one player from my youth, the legendary Hornets player Tyrone "Muggsy" Bogues. He is five foot three and was an amazingly quick guard who could run literal circles around men one to two feet taller than him. He worked hard and he played to his strengths of speed and dexterity. If he'd tried to be a center and make his career off his sexy dunks, he would have failed. But he didn't do that.

I'll say it again: *he worked hard to be the best he could.*

I've seen so many lazy talented people fail. Skills come to them effortlessly, but when they finally get challenged and have to work for something, they think something must be wrong.

Let's make up a scenario: Samantha is a painfully brilliant writer who won several literary contests in school. But when she started trying to publish professionally, she was suddenly up against other writers at the top of their games. She got three rejections. She tasted failure, decided that it was no fun, and quit.

Janice had okay grades, but wrote obsessively to improve her craft. She never won a literary competition and rarely got featured in her school's literary magazine. When she started trying to publish professionally, she got three rejections, but wasn't surprised, because nothing had come easy to her. She got another rejection, then another. Then a sale! Then three more rejections. Then things started going her way more often than not.

Who is the better writer? Or forget 'better'—who was more successful? Janice kept working because she knew that rejections happened. Samantha figured something was broken, either in her or in the system.

People who do the hard work instead of relying on talent will keep going when things are difficult. They're more likely to succeed.

BULLY: *Hey, wait a minute; didn't the author tell a story kind of like this in the intro? Writing was easy and fun until it got hard, so she quit?*

MUSE: *The point is that she got over it and kept going. Discouragement happens, but you have to get back up. She did. Eventually.*

All Writing Advice Is Crap

"Engrave this in your brain: EVERY WRITER GETS REJECTED. You will be no different. "

—John Scalzi,
award-winning science-fiction author

You may be asking how I can say writing advice is crap when I asked you to put down money for a book. Well, I admit the phrase is a little harsh, but many people (including myself) have looked at writing advice, realized it wouldn't work for them, and figured they were doing something wrong, not the writing advice.

Writing advice is generally trying to bring across good rules of thumb, but it's important to know yourself well enough to realize that when something doesn't work for you, you're allowed to try something else.

There is one piece of writing advice that you MUST follow: you have to write.

That's it.

IGNORE WRITING ADVICE

We all hit walls or get confused and end up needing advice here and there. That's what this book is for.

Many years ago, during my dry period, I was reading a popular writing book by someone considered a master of the craft. He said something about how you should love writing so much that if you didn't go leaping with joy to the typewriter every day, you weren't a real writer.

But that's just not how I roll. I don't love writing, per se. I love having written. I love looking at books on my shelf and knowing *I did that*. Sure, there are times that I get a rush when a plot point materializes in my head and I think, *I am doing the thing I was meant to do and it's wonderful*.

> **MUSE:** *That's where I have my time to shine!*

But more often I'm thinking, *Maybe I should do a whole bunch of other things beforehand. Oh look, it's dinnertime. I'll write tomorrow . . .*

> **BULLY:** *Where are you on those days, Muse? You're totally abandoning our hero here. She can't write without you.*

> **MUSE:** *She can. She does.*

I thought, if a master is telling me I'm going about this all wrong, then who am I to argue? I'm clearly not a writer. This fear fueled my inability to write for several years.

What I've learned since is that all writing advice should be taken with a grain of salt. Yes, even "show, don't tell," and "adverbs are evil."

Writing advice grows from the fertile fields of amateur writing. When beginning writers' stories are heavily laden with "she got angry," and "he said dumbly," we come up with advice to help the writers make it to the next level. We encourage them to describe *how* she got angry. Show the anger. Don't tell. We suggest that when you reduce the number of adverbs your writing will get stronger.

We say, "Don't edit the story at all until it's done," but then we hear pro authors say, "I edit the previous day's writing before I start on fresh words." They're doing that because they're professional writers. When beginning writers begin to fiddle and edit, then they more often than not get bogged down listening to the bully, struck with the desire to find the perfect word instead of just telling the story.

> **BULLY:** *I think my advice to find the perfect word is very good. Without the perfect words, the story is crap.*

If you can edit without getting bogged down, then edit before the story is over. If you can tell a descriptive story while using adverbs as the useful tools they are, then do it. If you understand why "she got angry" is weak writing but "she left the room" is fine, then don't worry about "show, don't tell."

BULLY: *I don't get it.*

MUSE: *Here's the clue: Show how her face is reddening and her hands are clenching. But don't show her hand closing around the doorknob and turning it. One helps the story along. The other slows it down.*

Avoid absolutes. If anyone—famous author, teacher, critique partner—tells you an absolute, such as "write every day" or "never edit until you're done" or "always write first thing in the morning when your mind is fresh," then step away slowly. Because some writers do just fine writing every couple of days, or binge writing on the weekend, or editing daily, or writing at lunch or after everyone goes to bed.

One of the things you must find out when you're writing is what works for you. As long as you're writing and finishing things, people can't tell you that you're doing it wrong.

And if you're holding tight to that adverb rule, go pick up a copy of any *Harry Potter* book. Rowling loves adverbs, and her books did just fine.

HABITS & ROUTINES

People of different minds require different inspirations when it comes to writing habits. I loved the idea of kicking my mind into "writing mode" in the morning when I had a fresh cup of coffee and the day ahead of me, with my little knitted Cthulhu doll on my desk cheering me on and my favorite writing music in my headphones. It's a great thing to build that "switch," and you can train your mind that it's writing time when you give it a ritual.

However, I dropped the idea of that cozy ritual when I was in a workshop where Cory Doctorow was teaching. He said sure, rituals were a great thing, but what happened when that routine was taken away from you? Does that mean you don't write when you travel? Does it mean you don't write when you run out of coffee?

Rituals can be useful. They help build habits. And if one helps you get started writing, great. But! If you don't tie yourself to a ritual, then you can write while at the airport, or on a train, or in your mother-in-law's house, or in the car (while someone else is driving, please). Nothing can stop you if you let go of your training wheels.

WRITING ADVICE:		**WRITING ADVICE:**
Picking up a habit is a great way to train your mind that it's time to write.		Avoiding habits is a great way to make sure you can write anywhere, anytime.

Now the big question: which works best for you? Establish your own process.

TRUSTING YOURSELF

Don't get tied to any piece of advice. Trust yourself. You may not write just like Ray Bradbury or J. K. Rowling or Stephen King, but if you write like yourself (and you *are* writing, which is the only rule), then you're doing just fine. Trust yourself and you can do this.

Setting goals is nearly always an absolute that can help you get disciplined with your writing, but what kind of goals work best for you?

Some people write to a word count: 250 words are considered a page. (That is, back when we used a monospace font, 12 point, double-spaced, on real paper.) A goal of 1,000 words is considered respectable, and 3,000 words usually is a standard chapter.

Some people write to a time limit. They can't get out of their desk chair until they've sat there with their empty page (Internet surfing doesn't count!) for half an hour, or an hour, or three hours.

Some people write to a chapter's end. Some days they'll write for an hour, getting 2,000 words. The next chapter will be longer, so they will write more, and on the short chapter days they write less. (**NOTE:** For this book I'm writing section by section. In fiction, I usually write to word count goals, but at the end of the book I will write until I am out of words for the day, with the momentum of a snowball rolling down a hill.)

Some authors write a specific word count or time length, to frightening precision. They stop when they reach the end, even if it's at the end of a sentence, and if they finish something before they've reached their limit, they start something new.

I can't say it enough. Trust yourself. Find what writing rules work for you. If you want to follow the standard rules, fine. If you want to break them, then see how that works out. If you're writing and finishing things, then you're heading in the right direction and no one can tell you otherwise.

PERFECTION
IS THE ENEMY

Let's dig a little deeper. Remember that thing I said earlier about how most people shouldn't edit when they write because that's all they will do? They will listen to that little bully on their shoulder that says they really need a better turn of phrase here, or they misused that word there, and should the story start here, or twenty years prior?

> **BULLY:** *All of those are completely valid questions. Second-guessing is the spice of life!*

People listen to the bully here because they think their story *has to be perfect.* They don't give themselves permission to write terrible, dreadful prose.

You don't want to write crap, though! You want to write stories that move mountains and start activism and redefine genres! Why would you actually set out to write crap?

First, you don't try to write crap. You just give yourself permission to write whatever comes to mind, with no judgment, if that's where the story goes.

Second, this is what editing is for. Fixing the crap.

Third, perfection is the enemy of the finished product.

Fourth, *it will never be perfect.*

The sooner you accept that, the happier you will be.

Let's go to a sports metaphor here. Let's say you want to run a marathon (and you're not already a runner). Maybe you admire certain runners. Maybe you figure it's a fun way to drop some weight. Maybe you're jealous of those little 26.2 magnets you see on people's cars. Whatever. You want to run a marathon!

If I told you that you had to go outside and run 26.2 miles tomorrow, and you'd better have a time that beats the last winner of the New York Marathon, you'd look at me as if I was wearing a strait jacket.

Of course you wouldn't go out expecting to run a marathon. The mind is just like this. Although it's not a physical muscle, it must learn like the rest of our bodies do: a little at a time, with repetition being key.

MUSE: *If I think we're going to just write all the words and rage-quit after an hour of failing, I'm less likely to come out again tomorrow!*

Here's another thing that may shatter some dreams: that great idea you have now? It probably won't sell.

Remember what I said about how ideas can't be copyrighted? You may have an awesome idea, but you probably don't have the skills to bring the idea to light. That's okay. You will develop these skills. But you have to let go of the dream of making your current idea perfect in order to develop those skills. You want to know what's so cool about being a creative person? The more ideas you develop, the more new ideas will come.

The new ideas often come when we're working hard on the existing ideas, buzzing around our heads like flies, saying, "No, pay attention to us! Not that story you're writing now!"

BULLY: *Every new idea is the best. You should work on the newest idea in your mind. Always.*

MUSE: *All those ideas are wonderful, like a bunch of ducklings chasing you! It means your creative mind is in overdrive, working hard! The important thing is to not be distracted.*

On one side, it's annoying to have your mind try to distract you from the work with a shiny new idea. On the other side, which is where I usually try to land, it's great to have so many story ideas.

Don't let them distract you. Just write them down in a notebook and promise yourself you'll get to them later.

Some people ask authors, "Where do you get your ideas?" Many authors want to know, "How do you make yours stop?" Ideas are never a problem for working writers.

I want to warn people, though, not to spend too much time on one project. I know so many people who have spent ten years on one novel, and that MUST BE the novel they sell. The idea of trunking it and moving on to another project is like quitting or giving up or failing in some way or another. They love their world and their characters. They are letting their friends down if they trunk the novel.

The problem here is that you can only get so much from one idea. You will learn more by writing two stories than by writing one and endlessly editing it. The thing is, there are no wasted words. I promise. That novel may not be saleable, but it will always be the first thing you finished, or the first time you really felt a connection with characters, and the next thing you write will be better because of it.

While climbing stairs, you don't look at the stairs below you and say, "Gee, those were wasted stairs." Of course not. You know you needed those stairs to get to where you are now. Every story that you don't sell—sometimes even the ones you don't finish—are that carry you toward being a better writer.

During that dry period I mentioned before, where I didn't write at all, I had a dream that was so sublime that I wanted to write it. Since I wasn't writing at the time, I just thought about the story. For years. Once I started writing again, I realized it was time to write the story just to get it out of my head. So I wrote it.

It was terrible. I sent it to a trusted friend and he tore it apart (metaphorically, and with professional kindness). But that was all right. I had written the story. It was out of my head. Sometimes I think maybe I'll write it better now, because I have a decade more of writing under my belt, but there are so many other ideas I want to write about that it's way down the list.

MUSE: *Here's a little secret: it's very hard to write your dreams into stories. Dreams are made of emotions and imagery that matter only to you, and when you try to translate those emotions with the imagery you've dreamed, you will likely fall short. That's not to say don't try it! But if you don't like what you come up with, remember that it's a lot tougher than you think it will be.*

Another thought on that perfection thing. Writing is subjective. This means that different people will get different things out of your story. So let's say you manage to attain that mythical perfect story you're yearning to write. You send it off in complete confidence. And it gets rejected.

Guess what? The editor didn't agree with you. It wasn't perfect to them.

Let's say the editor agrees with you! Buys the book! Sends it out to reviewers! And boom, it's eviscerated. It wasn't perfect to the reviewers. Readers give it one star. It lands on the Top Ten Most Disappointing Books of The Year lists!

MUSE: *I am pretty sure those don't exist.*

BULLY: *It's the Internet. Lists like that totally exist. Somewhere.*

So now you're confused and unhappy because the book was *perfect*! What happened? Do they hate you? Is there a vast global conspiracy against you?

No. Because there is no perfect book.

Your work won't get published if you wait for perfection. You write the best book you can and then you send it out and get to work on the next one. Don't edit the book once you send it out. Don't think about it. Just get back to work.

> **MUSE:** *Here's another secret: most of the time, your writer anxiety can be dealt with by getting back to work. Don't fuss on social media. Don't complain to friends. Just get back to work and write more.*

CHAPTER 5
Getting Started

> **Writers finish things. This was something told to me by one of my teachers. He said what separates people who want to write from writers is the fact that writers finish what they start. Where this really helps me is in the fight against 'the Shiny': I constantly battle ditching what I'm working on to run with the latest shiny idea that pops into my head. Every time I have to remind myself that 'writers finish things.' "**
>
> —**Maurice Broaddus,**
> fantasy and horror author

Y ou have your tools! You have put away your myths and locked the bully in a box where it will not be seen again! Now it's time to actually sit down and write!

But you have planes to catch and bills to pay and the cat's in the cradle and your favorite TV show is on! What now?

CHASING THE ELUSIVE TIME BEAST

The question I get more often than anything else is how to find time to write. As if time is something you can get at the store, as long as you can find the road to the store, or get the right link to buy online.

> **BULLY:** *You can't find time to write. You're far too busy with children, school, work, spouse, church, and volunteer work. Just give up.*

> **MUSE:** *You have the same amount of time per day as everyone else. If you can find time to watch TV, or play games, you can find time to write.*

How do you find time to write, though? There's work and school and family and commute and all those dogs to walk and cats to wax and fish to debone and birds to retrain to stop saying those words they've been saying since your cousin visited. Is writing below all of those important things?

But tell me this: do you have time to catch up on television? Do you have time to play tablet or phone games? Do you have time to text?

And heck, do you have time to clean? To cook? To ride the bus? To wait at a kid's soccer practice?

Writers do not have a time problem. We have a priority problem. When you sit down in front of the television, you're subconsciously saying, "I choose to do this instead of write."

Would you say that out loud?

Sometimes, maybe.

I understand the need to unwind after a hard day. I understand being physically and/or emotionally exhausted. But something has to give if you want to write. And when you list school, family, job, television, games, and naps, it's pretty clear which ones can be pushed aside for thirty minutes or so of writing.

We have the excuses. We all do. I've used them. *Can't write, I have kids.* Well, mothers and fathers have been able to write for years. Write when the kids are at school. Write at night. Put a movie on and write. Thirty minutes to an hour won't melt their brains.

Can't write, I have a day job. Well, Chuck Palahniuk wrote *Fight Club* while he worked at a gas station. Actually wrote it at work. He'd write a sentence or a paragraph, deal with a customer, and then write more.

BULLY: *Yeah, but Fight Club reads like that's how it was written.*

MUSE: *And it worked for that book. It was meant to be gloriously disjointed because of insomnia and the unreliable narrator. The point is, you can write anywhere, under any conditions.*

I can't fix your life for you and give you a magical hour to write. All I can do is tell you to take a hard look at your life and see where you can find thirty minutes. Ten minutes, even. Make a clear decision: what are you choosing to do—write or play games? Write or watch television? Write or sit waiting impatiently for an appointment?

So, what if you quit your job? Perhaps you think you are ready to retire or your spouse can carry the monetary load of the household. So many times, *so many times*, I have heard, "I wish I could just quit my job and write all day." You think if someone handed you eight hours then you could fill it with writing.

Sure, it's possible that can change your output. But in my experience, people find things to magically fill their free time. If I gave you eight hours, then the distractions that take away your writing time now will simply take away your writing time then, too.

I can speak from experience. I experienced the "lucky" position of the gift of time wrapped in a box of a corporate layoff. And suddenly the laundry became very important. Changing light bulbs are a huge priority. Groceries, man. They can take half a day.

I even made a rule for myself that I couldn't just fall back on computer games and television and reading when I was home. I had to do something as if I had a job. So I found housework to do. I found errands to run. I found emails to check and social media to respond to. My brain wanted to find anything that wasn't writing.

If you do not have the discipline to write right now, then you will not have the discipline to write when you have more free time.

So take thirty minutes before people get up in the morning. Take thirty after everyone goes to bed. Take your lunch hour. Write while dinner cooks. Write while the laundry dries. Write between classes. Any time where you reach for a fun distraction or rewarding relaxation moment, ask yourself whether you choose it over writing.

WRITER'S BLOCK

I sometimes joke on my podcast that professional writers can't get writer's block, because they have a job to do. Surgeons don't get surgeon's block and plumbers don't get plumber's block.

But the truth is, surgery and plumbing aren't creative pursuits, and we do sometimes just run up against a metaphorical wall in our writing and don't know what to do about it.

Continuing with the metaphor, you could keep hitting your head against the wall until it breaks (or your head does, and I know what I'm putting my money on in that fight), or you could find a way around it. Think Zen master, and how water can simply flow around a wall instead of trying to break through it.

Pretty imagery, yeah, but what the hell am I actually saying?

If you don't know where your story is going, then *write something else*.

Write a character's backstory. You might unearth something about him or her that can help you through the current problem. Write another chapter. No one said you have to write linearly. If you don't already have one, create an outline of the novel based on your existing chapters and see whether taking a step back will help you move ahead.

Or write another story.

Whatever you do, don't stare at the empty page. That is where madness lies.

Incidentally, I have successfully moved beyond a block in my writing by using all of the above methods. And the best part is, it feels really good to keep writing even though you're "stuck" somewhere. Continuing to write often helps you work around the problem, but you also develop confidence that the block didn't beat you, that you're still writing.

Even if the bully rears it's ugly head and begins to tell you that, sure—

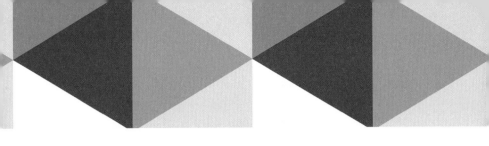

BULLY: *Sure, professional authors can get through this problem, but you're not a professional and therefore you can't do it. And even if you do, they will all find out you're a fraud anyway, because you are just a kid wearing an author's tweed jacket with suede elbow patches, puffing on a pipe.*

MUSE: *First, where did you get that vision of an author, 1965? We don't know any authors who look like that. And if you want to be a professional author, act like a professional author! That includes dealing with problems like a pro!*

BULLY: *And the tweed jacket.*

MUSE: *No tweed!*

As the Muse says, people who want to be pro authors "dress" like pro authors by acting with discipline when prioritizing their writing time. They write other things when stuck. And they keep going even when they feel like they're pretending and aren't really "real" writers.

YOU DON'T HAVE TO GO IT ALONE (NOT ENTIRELY)

Creative pursuits are always a lonely business. Even if you're collaborating with someone, there has to be time that you have to yourself, asking questions that only you can answer.

That doesn't mean you have to go it completely alone, though. If you're already itching to be a writer, it's likely you have found other people online or in meatspace who have the same desires and hopes and will like nothing more than sitting around and talking writing with you. You can discuss ideas, and writing processes, and complain about the latest rejection, how editors don't recognize your genius, and how the latest hit is really drivel and why can't everyone in the world see that?

But don't get me wrong—it really is lonely to write on your own and I totally know the lure of just being able to talk about your job at the watercooler like any office worker. Just remember that these sessions are about as much actual writing as a surgeon complaining about gallbladder removal is actual surgery.

MUSE: *This isn't writing.*

BULLY: *Nah, it's totally writing. It's thinking and planning and working hard. Complain about rejections and writer's block for a good afternoon—that's like finishing a whole short story!*

MUSE: *It really isn't.*

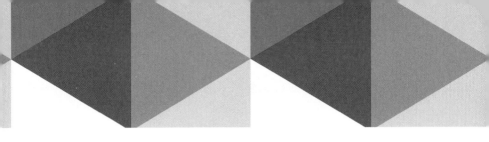

The time you will want to deal with other people who can completely change your writing career is in a good writing critique group. To find a good one that will help your career, make sure it hits some small and yet very important criteria. Such as:

Has anyone sold anything? To whom? It's not a deal breaker if you're all new writers, but a good group will have a gathering of people with different experience levels.

What are the rules of the workshop? Is there a minimum number of times you must submit to the group, or do the same people get reviewed every week and no one else submits? Are there guidelines on how to critique?

If you are interested in joining an existing group, try to subtly find out whether there is any existing group drama. Divas can rise in these groups, and some people could submit horrifyingly offensive/racist/sexist/homophobic stories every week, making everyone uncomfortable. (And they will never hear one word against these stories, interestingly enough.)

When dealing with a critique, I try to follow the rules for the workshops I had in grad school. They went like this:

People receive copies of the stories, and they read, comment on them, and write a short letter about what they took away from it. Then the group meets and the author must sit at the table and *remain silent* while everyone else talks about the story. They will talk about it as if they were a book club, with people getting a chance to bring up what they liked and what didn't work for them. If the group is large, or tends to be talkative, then the leader can have a time limit, giving the participants two or three minutes for their turn.

> **BULLY:** *That makes no sense. Why would you sit there while people attack your work? Stand up for yourself!*

> **MUSE:** *The people have to judge the story based on what you gave them. If you sold the story, then you wouldn't be able to go and knock on readers' doors and explain to them what you meant in this confusing part.*

After everyone has said their comments, the author is allowed to ask clarifying questions. "When you said you didn't like this character, can you be more specific?" "Did the ending fall flat because of this character's death, or was the pacing off?"

REMEMBER: Defending your story wastes everyone's time. They can't critique based on your intent. They critique based on what you gave them. If you didn't get your point across, and everyone pretty much agrees, then it's on you to decide to change it or not.

This sounds like I'm suggesting a dog pile. The critquers have jobs to do, too. They shouldn't give suggestions based on what they would do to fix the story. They should make sure they understand which story they're reading so that they don't recommend that your epic fantasy really needs a gumshoe detective and his nurse sidekick. It's their job to help you write the best story you can, not suggest how to make your story the best one they had a hand in.

Finding a critique group is a little harder if you're in a sparsely populated area or don't know a lot of authors, but there are still options:

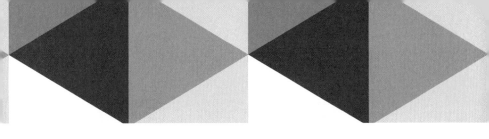

- Check your local library. Writing groups often meet there, and librarians might know a bit about your options.

- Check Meetup.com or other sites that bring groups of like-minded people together.

- If it's around November, check your area's forum on NaNoWriMo.org and see whether there are groups in your area meeting for write-ins. Go meet people and see whether they belong to writing groups that get together during other times of the year.

- And if none of that works, find an online workshop. Popular ones include Critters.org and Online Writers Workshops. These have intricate systems to make sure people don't abuse the arrangement and give only crappy critiques to others and demand good crits for themselves.

A note here about previously mentioned workshops that are more intensive: If you have the time and money to travel to a workshop, then by all means, take the opportunity. You will have a strong group of peers to relate to and well-respected authors, agents, and editors teaching you the tricks. These workshops cost money and time, though, so make your decisions carefully. Some workshops have scholarship programs, so look into those to see whether you are a good fit for one.

CHAPTER 6
Snips and Spice, Sugar and Snails

> " When I get stuck on a scene or I know it just isn't working, I often talk through the problem with a friend on chat, my family, or even a stuffed animal. It's magic! When you identify the problem well enough to describe it to someone else, you're also telling yourself what has to be done to fix it. "

—Andrea Phillips,
award-winning transmedia author

We're writing, right? But now we need to actually talk about the dang stories! Let's touch on the basics for a moment. What makes a story?

A story needs to have at least one character, a setting, a plot, and a conflict.

It doesn't necessarily need all of those things, and yes, experienced writers can experiment with artistic storytelling methods, but you must know the rules before you break them.

So let's talk about those rules.

CHARACTERS

These are the people in your story. Duh, right?

Slow down before you skip to the next part. Your characters need some nuance, not just warm bodies to carry your plot forward.

Your protagonist is often called your "hero" even though he/she may not always be a heroic figure who fights for good. The protagonist is the character who carries the action in the story, the one upon whose change the story's ending rests. A story usually makes a call for a protagonist to change. That doesn't mean the protagonist has to: if he or she doesn't or can't, then it's usually considered a tragedy.

Let's look at Shakespeare for some inspiration!

Much Ado about Nothing: Claudio changes by finding humility and is aghast at the supposed death of Hero, so he agrees to marry a stranger to make it up to Hero's family. He's rewarded with the realization that Hero is not dead, and the "stranger" he is marrying is, in fact, Hero. Beatrice and Benedict also agree to stop being so stubborn and admit their love for each other. They change, and are rewarded for it.

Othello: Othello can't see past his jealousy to the truth that his wife loves him, and he ultimately kills a whole bunch of people—except Iago, the antagonist who spread the lies about Othello's wife in the first place.

Macbeth: Macbeth and Lady Macbeth are both driven by hubris and ambition and refuse to back down, pushing them to kill again and again and letting guilt drag them both into madness.

MUSE: *"Tomorrow and tomorrow and tomorrow creeps in this petty pace from day to day, to the last syllable of recorded time."*

BULLY: *Macbeth really was a treat at parties.*

The person working against your protagonist is your *antagonist*. In basic terms, this person is often referred to as the villain, but that's not always the case. In a sports story, for example, you focus on one team and they will be the protagonists. The other team is often vilified to make for a better story, but really they're just around to stop the first team from winning, with rarely any ulterior motive (*The Karate Kid* notwithstanding). Sometimes we see a story from the villain's point of view, and the hero is the antagonist, trying to stop the protagonist from reaching his or her goal.

A very important thing to remember is only a shallow, cardboard antagonist has "destroy the protag" as his or her driving force. The antagonist is the hero of his or her own story, and she has his or her own wants and desires, too. In his or her story, the protagonist is his or her antagonist. To use the sports metaphor again, one team isn't good and one evil; they both just want to win.

The case of wanting something is key. Every character in your story needs to want something. This drives the plot forward. If your characters sit around just talking, and no one wants anything, then no one has a reason to get up out of his or her chair, or make that phone call, or fight that dragon. Even if a character wants a glass of water, it forces him or her to move. Even if he or she wants the other character to just get off his or her back and stop bothering him or her, it makes him or her act.

NOTE: The antagonist can also be anything from nature to society to the government. But more often than not, these larger establishments have someone representing them. The bank wants to foreclose on the house, but the bank is represented by a weasely little woman who revels in the small amount of power she has.

PLOT

"**P**lot" is what happens in your story. A simple way to think about at plot is that something in your character's world has changed, and she must either fight against that change or figure out how to incorporate that change into her life, but things will never be the same.

In *Star Wars*, Luke Skywalker's world changes when he buys stolen droids. You might think Hamlet's story begins when his father dies, but he really doesn't do anything about it until he sees his father's ghost. In my own *The Shambling Guide to New York City*, my character Zoe's story begins when she finds a strange job placement.

NOTE: The thing that changes your character's world may not be what you think it is. Hamlet's father dying is a huge thing that happens in his life, yes, but on stage his story starts when he sees his father's ghost. Something monumental can happen but people may manage to keep it hidden, or keep life the same. In Ada Palmer's *Too Like the Lightning*, the story doesn't begin with the criminal narrator's crimes. It doesn't begin when he meets the miraculous child he helps raise in secret. Instead, the story begins when someone else discovers the child, because that's when his world starts to unravel.

One could argue that the story for *Game of Thrones* begins twenty years prior when a king insults his wife and flirts with another woman at a tournament. But we don't see that; we see what happens years later when the secrets held about that time period begin to worm their way into the light.

> **BULLY:** *Look! I can quote literature, too! "You know nothing, John Snow."*

> **MUSE:** *Riiiight . . .*

Plot requires conflict, which is usually what happens organically when the antagonist moves to stop the protagonist from his or her goal.

SETTING

The setting is simply where the story takes place. It can be a living room or London or Westeros or a spaceship. Oftentimes a setting has a personality all its own; weather can affect a story. A labyrinth (literal, or just a poorly laid-out town or building) can slow characters down or put them in a place they didn't intend to go. Someone who doesn't know about the New York City Marathon or Chicago's St. Patrick's Day festivities could have a lot of trouble doing what the story needs done.

A good setting will make itself part of the story. The starship *Heart of Gold* in *The Hitchhiker's Guide to the Galaxy* is the future of space travel, and all the good and bad that brings with it. You can't forget the various castles in *Game of Throne*s. Or the sleek strict metal world that is the Death Star. (And if you want to talk settings as characters, I think the *Millennium Falcon* counts as a major character in most of the *Star Wars* movies.)

WARNING: Be careful when delving into description, though. If you're in love with your world so much that you spend more time describing how the afternoon's rain smells rather than how the hero felt when he fought with his mother, then you need to realign your priorities.

CHAPTER 7
Second Draft— Silk Purses from Sows' Ears

❝ I worry my imposter syndrome isn't as good as other people's. ”

—Ursula Vernon,
award-winning graphic novelist

Here's the bad news: come the second draft, you're not allowed to write garbage anymore. The second draft is when you go back and identify all the garbage.

> **BULLY:** *All of it. It's all garbage. Throw it out.*

> **MUSE:** *No, it's not garbage; it's a story that needs editing.*

I'm sorry I called it garbage. But the point is, the freewheeling, write-whatever-comes-to-mind time is over. Now the work begins.

FOUR STEPS TO EDITING SUCCESS

The one thing I don't like about editing advice is it's so "ten thousand feet," as the business world says. The advice is wide-sweeping and vague, and hard to actually do anything about. "Cut out passive voice," "raise the tension," "give the characters agency." What does any of that mean, and how do you deal with it?

I'm going to tell you how I edit. Some of these may seem like no-brainers, but when hospital workers are *reminded* to wash their hands, infection rates go down. That's all I'm saying.

Step 1

Before anyone sees my manuscript, I run a spelling and grammar check. Most word processors will have one. But pay attention! Sometimes the brilliant AI in Microsoft Word can't tell the difference between *its* and *it's*, or *there*, *their*, and *they're*. (Even spell checking THIS sentence, MS Word wanted to change some of those words.)

> **MUSE:** *Here's a little hint about the weirdness of English: 'It's' always means "it is." Always. So if you're talking about your dog Nellie and you mention "Nellie's ball," then Nellie gets an apostrophe. But if you don't know Nellie's name—*

> **BULLY:** *You don't know your own dog's name?*

> **MUSE:** *I'm saying this for the sake of the exercise! Anyway. If you don't know the dog's name, then you say "its ball"—no apostrophe. I didn't make the rules.*

If you write science fiction or fantasy, you will make your word processor curl up and cry when it has to tell you that every name you come up with is spelled incorrectly. Do it a favor and add your characters' names to the Ignore list.

Step 2

This one will require a bit more work. Do a search for the words *saw*, *heard*, *are*, and *was*. These verbs are considered weak.

> **BULLY:** *You JUST used the word 'are' right there!*

> **MUSE:** *Passive voice is a better match for nonfiction, as it's got a detached voice. Within fiction, a writer should avoid it.*

What does it mean that the verb is "weak"? I heard about these mysterious weak verbs long before someone told me what it meant.

Passive voice takes the object of the sentence and puts it in the place of the subject. We consider a sentence like "The alien ate his face" to be active. The subject, the alien, does the verb, eating, to the object, his face. To make that sentence weaker, we say, "His face was eaten by the alien." Now the focus isn't on the active subject but instead on the passive object.

> **MUSE:** *Passive voice is great in politics when you don't want to name a scapegoat. President Ronald Reagan's famous statement "Mistakes were made" is a great use of passive voice. It cuts the subject out altogether so we focus on the mistakes and not **who** made them. If you're writing about politicians, passive voice in your dialogue can actually be a clever too*

What about the *saw* and *heard* verbs? How can we describe what our character sees and hears?

This is a point-of-view issue. Nellie the dog is in a room about to have an exciting scene. You're seeing the scene from her point of view. So you could write, "Nellie heard a thump, and then saw the alien burst into the room. She heard it screaming." That's a lot of words!

But because we're already in Nellie's point of view, it's not confusing at all to say, "Something thumped on the door, and then the alien burst into the room, screaming and waving its tentacles." We lost nothing of the information, and the sentences are tighter and more exciting.

Find your passive verbs and rewrite those sentences to be more active.

Step 3

Now we are at the point where we need to read for clarity and continuity.

Did you change your protagonist's name halfway through? Did the color of Nellie's collar change after the encounter with the alien? Did her owner, Jermaine, lose his dominant arm in Chapter 2 and then throw the ball with Nellie in Chapter 4?

This is challenging, and not something you can skim for. A minor example: I changed a scene from taking place on a long ladder to taking place in an elevator. Search for the words ladder and rung, change those sentences to reference elevators, and I'm covered, right? Nope. When you're on a ladder talking to people, you're going to look straight up or straight down to address them. That doesn't make sense in an elevator. The dialogue was super weird. Luckily, the copyeditor caught that one.

During this sweep, you will find awkward phrasing and the like that you'll want to change. So do it. Now is the perfect time.

If you have time, read some of your story aloud. Nothing makes bad sentences stand out like reading them aloud. It's worth the time.

Step 4

Time to find some readers. If you have a writers' group or some friends, get them involved. Tell them you want an alpha read or a beta read.

Writers request an alpha read when they want to make sure the structure of the story is sound. Does it make sense that these things happen in this order? Think about it as someone checking your house's foundation. The contractor is not going to give a crap what color your carpets are, and he may not even care if a window is broken. He is just there to check the structure of the house.

If you're happy with that, then you can ask for a beta read, which is a deeper read. These readers act as an editor, looking for weak spots, continuity errors, factual errors, and the like.

They will come back with suggestions. It's your job to put on your big writer's pants and take the criticism. They want to make your book better. If you are just sending it to them asking for validation of your perfect writing, then you're wasting your time and theirs.

Sometimes writers will get critiques that they want to follow but just can't figure out what the reader means. Here are some explanations of common comments:

AGENCY: Writers often make the mistake of focusing totally on their protagonist and antagonist, and all other characters are satellites, orbiting the story, stuck in the gravitational pull. For your characters to have agency, they have to make choices. If they are ordered to do something, if they are forced to do something, they have no agency. If the girlfriend does what the hero says, goes back home and cries and looks pretty and does nothing else for the entire story, then she has no agency. If she refuses to do what he says, or decides to go back home on her own, she is making choices. Does she do her own stuff to hinder the antagonist? Does she send reinforcements to the hero without his asking for it? Does she leave him because she's sick of him chasing adventure and getting himself injured and then she has to take care of him? That's agency.

The use of gendered pronouns is no accident here; women in stories often have the least agency. A saying goes, if you can replace a woman with a sexy lamp and the story stays exactly the same, then she has no agency. (Incidentally, this is why I don't like the movie *The Princess Bride*. Buttercup makes zero decisions; she just does what every man in the story requires of her. If the men were fighting over the best sexy lamp in the kingdom, the movie would be largely unaltered. The only time she shows a backbone is when she is about to attempt suicide, but Wesley stops her, because God forbid she injure her boobs.)

RAISING TENSION: Sometimes called "upping the stakes," this means that the characters have little plot reasons pushing them along other than "it fits the story." People must want something when they make decisions, and that "want" can be to get a glass of water. If they're jogging, it's to prepare for a race, and if they're running, it's to get away from a dog.

This came up in a project of mine, where one character was trying to encourage her friend to take a job that the friend didn't really want. The first character had something driving her: she didn't want her friend to be unemployed. But my agent suggested that the character didn't have enough incentive to be "helping" her friend find employment. In real life, you help a friend just because it's kind. In a story, though, it's always better for someone to have additional motivation. I decided that the first character had a deadline to fill that job posting or else she'd lose her own job. Now she was more likely to push her friend into a job she may hate, but hey, she's "helping" her friend get a job, right?

The scenes don't need to be exciting to up the stakes. In one book of George R.R. Martin's series, *A Song of Ice and Fire* (*Game of Thrones* on TV), the women of the castle drink wine while war wages on outside. They don't see the war; no one is attacking them (yet). But they know that their loved ones are in danger. And they know if their defenders fall, then they are going to be killed or captured. The queen tells dreadful stories of her youth and gets drunker and drunker, while young Sansa feels helpless, stuck inside with a drunk, monstrous queen, and knowing that if she goes outside, death awaits her.

MUSE: *Sansa Stark is a fascinating character if you want to discuss agency. Some may argue she has none until much later, but she does; she just makes **bad** decisions. That's still having agency.*

PERFECTION: Scrub this word from your vocabulary right now. Unless you use it in a book, don't even think it. Nothing will ever be perfect; it will just be done. You can write the best book, and rewrite it, and get notes back from editors, and rewrite it again, and have more professional editors pore over it, and then when it goes out, it will still have errors. It happens. Let go of the perfection curse: just like with your first draft, if you worry about your later drafts being perfect, you will never send it out.

Ever.

Voltaire said, "Perfect is the enemy of the good." Don't shoot for perfect. Good is good enough.

CHAPTER 8

Let It Go

> **Building your own platform will create opportunities for you in mainstream publications. The more you are your own PR machine, the better your chances of success. "**
>
> **—Mikki Kendall,**
> comics and nonfiction writer

I am prone to earworms, so this chapter was murder for me, but we push onward. It's an important lesson all writers need to know, once we actually finish something.

What happens when we are finally, officially, done with our edits? The next step is perhaps the most frightening thus far: you have to open your metaphorical window, put your carefully cupped hands outside, and let your work fly away. And once it's gone, it's no longer in your control.

All right, you can control a bit of it. First, you have two options: self publishing and traditional publishing. And within those paths, you can choose where you place your work, who to work with (sometimes), and how much to charge for it (sometimes). The big thing you can't control is how people will read your work.

So to take this big step, you have to ask yourself one of the questions I receive more than many others: When you let your work go, should you go the DIY route, or work with an agent and publisher?

TRADITIONAL PUBLISHING

Back in the day, a writer would go to the library and get the *Writer's Market*, a massive book with exhaustive lists of all the agents and magazine and book publishers in the business. You would search through and pick out some agents to submit to, follow their guidelines, send out some submissions, eventually sign with one, who would then send your book out to publishers. It was clean and tidy.

Nowadays, you probably won't find one writer with a story like that. Or like anyone else's.

My many-year story went like this:

1. Tried to get an agent, failed, submitted a book, failed, decided to self-publish it via podcast.

2. Successful podcast gets agent #1's attention, I signed with him, and then he never returned my calls or emails about my book. I fired him.

3. Agent #2 I got through a mutual friend, but she couldn't sell the book I wrote. She fired me.

4. Agent #3 pursued me after a successful Kickstarter campaign to self-publish some popular podcast novellas. She wanted to sell those books, not the one I was writing at the time. I ended up selling the book on my own after chatting with an editor at a convention and sending it to her directly. Agent #3 quit being an agent and then passed me to her boss, Agent #4. So now #4 and I were in a relationship that neither of us chose.

5. Agent #4 also thought the work I did years and years ago was the one we should sell, despite the fact that I was sick of it after constant editing on different agents' recommendations. We parted ways after I asked her whether she cared about anything I was writing at the time, and she said no. (The conversation was more professional that that, for what it's worth.)

6. Agent #5 I met at a convention. When Agent #4 and I parted ways, I contacted #5. We are still together; finally I got into a relationship that works.

None of these situations was a "shady character takes advantage of poor defenseless author" arrangement. They were just relationships that didn't work.

We joke that the agent/client relationship is like a marriage, but it really is. You may meet some agents that seem good and turn out to be bad relationships. You can only work with one (without getting into trouble!). And if you want to get a divorce, it's very bad form to have someone lined up to take his or her place once it's over. You search for a new agent after you've parted ways with the old. If you find a new agent soon after your "divorce," it's not considered unprofessional, but just make sure you weren't looking for someone while you were with your old agent.

What does an agent do for you? So many people think that agents are just there to take 15 percent of your sales, but I am very glad to have my agent. Here's a list of what she does for me:

- Uses connections at publishing houses to introduce my work, which lets my books get faster attention than a book on the slush pile. (Also, some houses won't look at unagented submissions at all.)

- Looks over my contracts for clauses that do not serve me.

- Argues/negotiates on my behalf about contracts and other issues with the publisher/editor.

- Works with me to brainstorm new ideas and whom to send them to.

- Gets my proposals and books to make sure they're the best they can be before we pitch to editors.

- Talks me down from the cliff's edge if the bully is making me doubt all of my choices in life.

- Connects me with foreign rights opportunities by getting my book in front of international publishing houses.

- Connects me with film rights opportunities by getting my book in front of movie producers.

So if you're wondering whether that is worth 15 percent of your income, trust me. It is.

Now the other half of the pro world is the editor and publishing house. The editor has the opportunity to buy your book, but she's not the only person who has to say yes. First she has to like it, and then she has to convince sales and marketing that it's a good risk to take. You may find an editor who loves your work, but if she can't convince others to get on board, then you're sunk.

So the editor and the publishing house love the book and make an offer. Here is where things get dicey, and we don't have a lot of room to go into the nitty-gritty. (This is why having an agent is good!)

The offer is considered an advance, which means they are guessing you will earn at least that much once the book comes out, and you will make maybe 8 percent of every book sold. For low advances, you'll have to sell fewer books to earn out, and the bonus here is less pressure. Higher advances have more pressure to sell thousands and thousands of copies to earn out, or your next advance won't be as big.

BULLY: *Wait, go back. I get 8 percent of the cover price? Seriously? That's sick! That's MY money!*

MUSE: *You're not working solo anymore. Your editor and cover designer and layout and sales force and assistants and others all get their income from your book sales, too. Not to mention you have to pay for printing the books. It's a give-and-take thing. You take their services and give them part of the book's income.*

Most self-publishing sites work on the same principle: in the US, for example, if your book costs less than $3, you get 30 percent of the cover price; otherwise, you get 70 percent.

Another thing a traditional publisher will give you is an advance in one lump sum, and unless you don't deliver the book, you don't have to give that back. They also get the book in front of more people via book shelves, reviews, and marketing. Unless you're a breakout hit, the self-pub income is almost always less than the lump sum of an advance.

The dark side of big advances is that the expectation is much higher and it may take a long time to earn out. However, as long as you deliver the book, you don't have to pay the advance back even if it never earns out.

As the muse said, traditional publishing offers a team of people working with you to make the book better. Right now, I'm looking at words on a computer screen, but a publishing house will turn that into a nicely laid-out book or a tidy e-book or a highly produced audiobook. I will turn in something with no pictures and no cover art, and there will be typos everywhere. Once I get it back, it will have been edited for content, copyedited, laid out, printed (or converted, or produced in a studio), with a professionally designed cover, and others will probably have heard of it due to the work of the marketing department. If I get any *Publishers Weekly* or *Kirkus* reviews, that will be due to my publisher as well. And then it gets into stores with no effort at all from me.

If I self-publish, I have to be responsible for the layout and editing and cover art and uploading to stores. It's extremely unlikely I'll get professional journal reviews. It's a great deal of work, and if something goes wrong like a misprinting (if I'm making physical copies of my book), then it's my responsibility to fix. (This has happened to me. I have a lot of misprinted books in my basement!)

So why self-publish?

SELF-PUBLISHING

It is so much easier now to self-publish your work. Over the past decade, the world has changed to give writers more power than ever before.

You self-publish to have total control over all elements of the project. No one will slip a crappy cover on your book unless you say it's okay!

Your income can be anywhere between 30 and 70 percent of the cover price, and you get paid either monthly or quarterly.

You publish on a schedule you choose. If you can write it and produce it in a month, you can publish it in a month. Traditional houses take anywhere from twelve to eighteen months from contract to shelf.

As of this writing, popular self-publishers are Amazon, Smashwords, and Payhip. Most of these work on the same principle: if your book costs less than $3, you get 30 percent of the cover price; otherwise, you get 70 percent.

You can find out all of this information in each site's terms and conditions, which are often irritating to study but so important. This is your intellectual property you're dealing with here, and you have to be your own agent and make sure you're not getting hit with an unexpected contractual trap.

Resources are available for you to hire cover artists, graphic designers, and copyeditors if you don't want to do that yourself (and goodness, those who do have my respect!). Check out the message boards on the site where you want to publish. The Kindle forums have a lot of information on people who can help out with your self-publishing efforts.

Unless you're an outlier, your income will probably not be mind-blowing, but you can make a nice amount with self-pub, and getting paid more often is very useful.

I've talked mostly about e-books here, but you can also print books and sell them. Lulu and CreateSpace are good sites to print your own books, and print-on-demand (POD) makes it relatively affordable because you don't have to keep 5,000 books in your garage where the humidity and mice will ruin them anyway.

You can also serialize on a blog, via crowdfunding sites like Patreon, or even give away subscriptions to print or audio serializations via podcast. Incidentally, releasing my work via audio podcast was how I built my audience. I released them for free, but it paid off in the end, big time.

The best thing about being alive in today's publishing waters is there are so many options for an author, whether you go traditional, self, or some kind of hybrid option. The key is to research all of your options to find the best for you. If you prefer to sit back and let others deal with the nonwriting bits, then go traditional. If you want total control and more money, go self-pub.

In Closing

It's a tough world out there, with the stresses of writing, editing, submitting, and deciding the future of your book. And chances are good that for a long time you would make more money doing almost any other job out there. But if you've made it this far and you're still thinking that storytelling is something that is in your blood, and you would be lost without it, then you're a writer.

Those monsters outside your door can't defeat you! With your trusty sword and shield (metaphors for pretty much anything involving the writer's life) you will conquer them, slaying the beasts that wish to drag you down, tell you that you're crap, insist that others are better, and promise you that you'll never make it.

If you only take one thing away from this book, please let it be the faith that persistence will pay off. If you keep writing, and keep working to grow as a writer, then you will succeed. It will probably take a while, but that's okay. Most things worth doing take a very long time. Be persistent. Be strong. Because you should be writing.

Resources

I'd love to tell you that this book is the only resource you'll need as a writer. But as I said, not everyone writes the same way, and finding the support and inspiration that works best for you is important.

Here are some other writing resources that you might find helpful. Some of them are time-honored publications that every writer has heard of, while others are contemporary underground writing hubs run by foul-mouthed veterans. Take a moment to check these resources out and continue your education and grow as a writer. Great work doesn't occur in a vacuum.

BLOGS

Chuck Wendig's *Terrible Minds*, www.terribleminds.com/ramble/blog
Kameron Hurley, www.kameronhurley.com
Andrea Phillips, www.deusexmachinatio.com
John Scalzi, www.whatever.scalzi.com

PODCASTS

Writing Excuses
The Roundtable
The Creative Penn
Grammar Girl's Quick and Dirty Tips for Better Writing
    (already on the list, but please fix the name)
The Narrative Breakdown
The Creative Writer's Toolbelt
The Narrative Breakdown
Critiki Party
Odyssey Podcasts
Shipping & Handling Podcast
Get To Work, Hurley
And of course, *I Should Be Writing* and *Ditch Diggers!*

BOOKS

Booklife by Jeff VanderMeer
Wonderbook by Jeff VanderMeer
Save the Cat! by Blake Snyder
45 Master Characters by Victoria Schmidt
On Writing by Stephen King
Storyteller by Kate Wilhelm
Beginnings, Middles & Ends by Nancy Kress
The War of Art by Steven Pressfield
The Hidden Tools of Comedy by Steve Kaplan
Writing the Other by Nisi Shawl and Cynthia Ward
Steering the Craft by Ursula K. Le Guin

MAGAZINES

The Writer
Writer's Digest
Writer's Market
Poets and Writers
Scratch
Bodega Magazine
Kill Your Darlings
Writers' Forum
Publishers Weekly
Self Publishing Magazine

Care & Feeding of Your Author

Congratulations! You're the new owner of a baby writer! If you take good care of it, then it will live a long, happy life. But there are some rules!

To hatch the new writer, give it a pencil and a notebook. If it gives you an annoyed look, then put it in front of a computer with a word processor.

Once it's hatched and free of its egg, make sure it gets regular exercise. Note that this means short, regular visits to the notebook or computer. Do not starve the baby writer by keeping away too long, and do not exhaust it by binge writing 10,000 words at a time.

Your writer will need love. It won't understand at first that the quality of its writing isn't what's important. You don't require baby eagles to soar, or baby humans to perform complex—or even simple—math problems. Why would you expect your baby writer to write Pulitzer-level work? Remind the baby writer of this. Put words on the page: that's all that's required, baby writer.

When the baby writer is fussy, then check three things: Is it hungry? Writers often ignore food when they're writing too much. Is it sleepy? Lack of sleep makes everyone from babies to old people cranky, and writers are not immune. If it's writing too late into the night, urge it to get some sleep and the world will look brighter.

Is it smelly? Make it take a shower, cause dang, you gotta take care of yourself, baby writer. Don't be the smelly kid.

Can your writer walk and talk on its own? Is it running around the playground, climbing to the top of the slide and writing fanfic of television shows that aren't even on the air anymore? It might be time for some more official schooling. Think about taking it to a convention or a workshop or just somewhere that it can meet other writers. Socialization is important. You wouldn't want your unsocialized writer to start biting other writers.

If you're feeding your writer regularly with words, food, sleep, and showers, and giving it some friends to play with every once in a while, then you and your writer should have a long and happy life! Have fun!

Writing Exercises

All right, enough talk—let's write.

Here you'll find several exercises that will test your versatility, creativity, and hard writing work. These should be both a way to flex your writing muscle and a good time.

After some basic writing prompts, you'll find ones referencing your story, or your protagonist, or your setting. These can be whatever you want them to be—are you pulling characters from a story you've already written? Are you creating new ones off the top of your head? Are you writing fanfiction, using characters from other media? Have fun with it.

Take your time with these writing prompts, and have fun. Don't think of this as a final exam, but an exciting new beginning, a chance to show what you've learned from reading this book.

Go ahead. You've got this. I believe in you.

Writing Exercise

MAKE A LIST OF EVERY REASON YOU HAVE NOT TO WRITE.

Writing Exercise

10 STORY IDEAS IN 10 MINUTES. GO!

Writing Exercise

TAKE A LINE OF POETRY OR A LINE FROM A SONG AND SEE
WHAT KIND OF STORY IDEA YOU CAN COME UP WITH.
(EXAMPLE: Shakespeare is by far the most popularly used bard,
as in *The Sound and the Fury*.)

Writing Exercise

TAKE A LONG SHOWER OR GO FOR A LONG DRIVE. CLEAN THE FLOORS. WHATEVER YOU DO, DON'T PLAY MUSIC OR WATCH TV OR HAVE ANY DISTRACTIONS. SEE IF YOU CAN COAX YOUR MUSE OUT TO PLAY. WHEN YOU'RE DONE, WRITE DOWN EVERY IDEA YOU GOT.

Writing Exercise

LOOK AT THE NEWS. COME UP WITH FIVE STORY IDEAS "RIPPED FROM THE HEADLINES." WRITE A STORY ABOUT SOMEONE INTERVIEWED IN THE NEWS. WRITE A STORY ABOUT SOMEONE AFFECTED BY THE STORY. WRITE ONE WHERE SOMEONE BENEFITS FROM THE RESULT OF THE NEWS COVERED.

(Bonus if the news is tragic. Who benefits from a fire or a murder?)

Writing Exercise

TAKE A HISTORICAL FIGURE AND CHANGE SOMETHING FUNDAMENTAL ABOUT HIM. WHAT IF HITLER WERE A WOMAN? WHAT IF MARIE CURIE WERE LATINA? WHAT IF GENGHIS KHAN WERE GAY?

Writing Exercise

READ. PICK UP SOMETHING OUTSIDE YOUR GENRE. BONUS IF IT'S A BOOK YOU DON'T THINK YOU'LL LIKE. DON'T HATE-READ; READ WITH THE INTENT THAT YOU ARE GOING TO LEARN SOMETHING. EVEN IF THE BOOK IS TERRIBLE, WHAT CAN YOU LEARN FROM IT TO ENHANCE YOUR OWN WRITING?

Writing Exercise

THE CONSPIRACY THEORISTS AND TINFOIL-HAT-WEARERS WERE RIGHT, AND THAT THING THEY WARNED ABOUT COMES TRUE.

Writing Exercise

WRITE SOME FANFIC ABOUT YOUR FAVORITE BOOK OR MOVIE.
EMBRACE IT. HAVE FUN WITH IT. KEEP TELLING THE STORIES
OF THESE BELOVED CHARACTERS. (DON'T SELL IT.)

Writing Exercise

WRITE A DINNER SCENE WITH A FAMILY THAT HAS AN "ELEPHANT IN THE ROOM" BUT REFUSES TO TALK ABOUT IT. IS SOMEONE MISSING BECAUSE SHE'S IN JAIL, OR BECAUSE OF A FALLING-OUT FROM LAST YEAR? HOW CAN YOUR CHARACTERS TALK ABOUT IT WITHOUT TALKING ABOUT IT? WHAT CAN YOU USE TO RATCHET UP THE TENSION IN THE ROOM?

Writing Exercise

A CIRCUS PERFORMER RUNS AWAY TO JOIN A CORPORTAION.
THE GRASS IS ALWAYS GREENER. GO WITH THIS IDEA.

Writing Exercise

WHAT DOES YOUR SETTING BRING TO YOUR STORY?
WRITE A SCENE WHERE THE SETTING IS KEY. IF THE
SAME CHARACTERS HAD THE SAME PROBLEM IN A
DIFFERENT PLACE, WHAT WOULD BE DIFFERENT?

Writing Exercise

PEOPLE'S WISHES START COMING TRUE—BUT THEY ONLY GET ONE WISH IN THEIR LIFETIME. AND THEY DON'T KNOW WHEN IT WILL HAPPEN. "I WISH FOR WORLD PEACE" IS NICE, BUT PEOPLE ARE MORE LIKELY TO SAY SOMETHING LIKE, "I WISH YOU WOULD LISTEN TO ME" OR "I WISH YOU WOULD GO AWAY." WHAT HAPPENS TO YOUR PROTAGONIST?

Writing Exercise

A WAITER IS ON HIS FIRST DAY AT WORK. HE NERVOUSLY SPILLS A GLASS OF ICE COLD WATER DOWN THE BACK OF SOMEONE AT A TABLE. WRITE ONE PARAGRAPH WHERE THIS HAPPENS TO YOUR PROTAGONIST. THEN WRITE A SIMILAR PARAGRAPH FOR EACH MAIN CHARACTER.

(HINT: Each character should respond differently to this experience.)

(Continued on the next page)

Writing Exercise

THE BEST VILLAINS ARE SYMPATHETIC IN SOME WAY. WHAT ASPECT DOES YOUR VILLAIN HAVE THAT MAKES HER MORE LIKABLE? (HINT: Someone could have abused her, or he could be extremely talented at doing something, or she shows kindness or love toward someone other than your protagonist.)

Writing Exercise

WEATHER CAN BE OVERUSED TO SET MOODS. AND THEN AGAIN, IT COULD HAVE A STORY RELY ENTIRELY ON IT ("TO BUILD A FIRE" BY JACK LONDON, "JUST LIKE THE ONES WE USED TO KNOW" BY CONNIE WILLIS, AND "ALL SUMMER IN A DAY" BY RAY BRADBURY ARE GOOD ONES). WRITE A SCENE WHERE THE WEATHER DRIVES THE CONFLICT.

Writing Exercise

WHAT CAN EVERYONE AROUND YOUR CHARACTER DO THAT THEY CAN'T DO? HOW DO THEY FEEL ABOUT THIS?

Writing Exercise

YOUR PROTAGONIST AND ANTAGONIST HAVE SOMEONE IN THEIR LIVES
THAT COULD PROBABLY SWAY THEM FROM THEIR PATH. WHO IS THAT
WHAT WOULD THAT PERSON SAY TO MAKE THEM DO SO?

Writing Exercise

TAKE A SCENE FROM YOUR STORY WHERE YOUR CHARACTER
IS FACING SOMETHING DIFFICULT. MAKE IT HARDER. WE DON'T
LIKE CHARACTERS THAT OVERCOME EASY OBSTACLES.
READERS WANT TO ROOT FOR THEIR HEROES.

141

Writing Exercise

GIVE YOUR PROTAGCNIST HER GREATEST DESIRE, BUT IN A "MONKEY'S PAW" KIND OF WAY. SHE GETS TO SPEND HER LIFE WITH HER TRUE LOVE—BUT SHE'S MARRIED TO HIS SIBLING. SHE GETS HER DREAM JOB BUT NEVER GETS CREDIT.

Writing Exercise

YOUR CHARACTER INHERITS A BOX FROM A RELATIVE.
INSIDE IS THE FINAL PIECE TO EVERY JIGSAW PUZZLE
SHE HAS EVER DONE. THE PIECES FIT TOGETHER.

Writing Exercise

EVERYONE HAS A PRICE, SOMETHING THAT WOULD CORRUPT
HIM OR HER. WHAT IS YOUR PROTAGONIST'S?

Writing Exercise

YOUR ANTAGONIST IS INTERRUPTED FROM HIS DASTARDLY DEEDS BY A PHONE CALL FROM A PARENT.

Writing Exercise

SOMEONE DISCOVERS THAT HER NEMESIS HAS A
SECRET ONLINE IDENTITY, ONLY INSTEAD OF A TROLL,
THE NEMESIS IS A PHILANTHROPIST.

Writing Exercise

MIDWAY THROUGH A FIGHT, THE PROTAGONIST AND ANTAGONIST KISS. WHAT'S THE FIRST THING SAID WHEN THEY BREAK APART?

Writing Exercise

DO A SEARCH IN YOUR STORY FOR SENTENCES CONTAINING THE WORDS *LOOKED, HEARD, SAW, FELT*, AND *WAS*. TIGHTEN EACH SENTENCE YOU FIND.

(EXAMPLE: "She heard an owl call in the woods," becomes "An owl broke the silence with its screech, startling her.")

Writing Exercise

ONE OF THE CHARACTERS YOU'VE WRITTEN ABOUT IN THIS BOOK WALK INTO THE ROOM, STARTLING YOU AS YOU READ THIS. WHAT HAPPENS?

Writing Exercise

STUCK? GO FOR A WALK. THINK ABOUT YOUR CHARACTERS'
FAVORITE CLOTHING. THINK ABOUT THEIR PASTS. WONDER WHAT
THEY WOULD SAY IF THEY WERE WALKING WITH YOU. DON'T
THINK ABOUT WHAT YOU'RE STUCK ON, BUT CREATE
NEW IDEAS INSTEAD. NOW WRITE THEM DOWN.

Acknowledgments

Thanks to James Patrick Kelly for his continued advice and support, my agent Jennifer Udden, and Rage Kindelsperger and Chris Krovatin from Quarto. I'd like to recognize my mentors through the years, including Richard Dansky, David Anthony Durham, Elizabeth Hand, Nancy Holder, and Cory Doctorow. And of course my friends the old school podcasters: Christiana Ellis, Evo Terra, Mike Mennenga, Dave Slusher, Summer Brooks, Tee Morris, Pip Ballantine, Scott Sigler, A Kovacs, and my partner in podcasting crime, Matt Wallace.

And as always, my parents, Will and Donna, and my husband, Jim, and daughter, Fiona. I love you all so much.